# EPIC FUN WITH RAMAYANA

Akshata Satish

Clever Fox® PUBLISHING

Chennai • Bangalore

CLEVER FOX PUBLISHING
Chennai, India

Published by CLEVER FOX PUBLISHING 2025

ISBN: 978-93-6707-104-5

# "The King Who Wished For Children"

Long ago, in Ayodhya, the capital of the Kosala kingdom, lived a kind king named Dasharatha. He had three queens, Kausalya, Sumitra, and Kaikeyi. He had everything he could wish for, yet he was sad because he had no children. One day, Sage Vashishta visited the palace. The king told him he wished for children. The sage advised him to perform a special prayer called the Putrakameshti Yagna. Feeling hopeful, the king invited Sage Rishyashringa to perform the yagna.

## "Yagna Time: Find the Right Items!"

**INSTRUCTIONS:** Look at all the pictures below. Some things are needed for a yagna, and some are not. Circle the items that are needed for a yagna. Cross ✗ out the ones that are not needed

# "Arrival of the Princes"

Upon the successful completion of the yagna, Agni (god of fire) appeared from within the yagna fire and handed over the blessings in the form of sweet kheer (rice pudding). Soon, the royal family was blessed with four baby boys. Queen Kausalya gave birth to Rama. Queen Kaikeyi gave birth to Bharata. Queen Sumitra gave birth to twins, Lakshmana and Shatrughna. The entire kingdom of Ayodhya rejoiced at the birth of these four princes.

# "Princes and Cradles"

**INSTRUCTIONS:** Find out which cradle belongs to which prince by following the correct path through the maze.

# "The Childhood of the Princes"

The four brothers loved playing in the palace garden, pretending to be warriors with wooden swords. Lakshmana always stayed with Rama, while Shatrughna followed Bharata. As they grew older, they were sent to Sage Vashishtha's ashram to study scriptures, math, royal duties, and combat skills. They also learned values like truth, kindness, and dharma to prepare for their future as noble rulers.

## "Find the hidden objects and Color"

# "The Journey with Vishwamitra"

One day, Sage Vishwamitra visited King Dasharatha's palace and asked for his help. He said, "I am performing a yagna, but two evil demons, Maricha, and Subahu, keep disturbing it. I cannot curse or kill them, as it is against the rules to do so during a yagna. I need Rama to protect the ritual." King Dasharatha was worried. He said, "Rama is still young. Instead, I will send my army to protect you or I will lead the battle!" But Sage Vashishta assured him that Rama was no ordinary boy, and he is born for a great purpose. Hearing this, Dasharatha finally agreed. Rama and Lakshmana left with Sage Vishwamitra.

## "Fill in the blanks"

1.Sage ____________________________ came to the palace.

2.He asked for ________________________ to protect the yagna.

3.Rama and ________________________ went with the sage.

4.Two demons named _________________ and _________________ were disturbing the yagna.

5._________________ persuaded Dasharatha to send Rama with Vishwamitra

# “Defeat of demons”

As they journeyed through the forest, Sage Vishwamitra taught Rama sacred mantras and gifted him divine weapons (astras). The next day, the yagna began, and Rama and Lakshmana stood guard. Soon, the demons appeared and started disrupting the ritual. Rama and Lakshmana fought fearlessly and defeated Tataka, Subahu and Maricha, proving their strength and courage.

# “Divine gifts to Rama”

**INSTRUCTIONS:** Rama received magical weapons from Sage Vishwamitra. Read each name and match it to the correct description by drawing a line.

| | |
|---|---|
| Vayavyastra | Unleashes blazing fire |
| Chandrastra | Counters serpent weapons |
| Agneyastra | Emits light and scorching heat |
| Varunastra | Controls the wind |
| Garudastra | Moon weapon for calming |
| Nagastra | Summons great floods |
| Suryastra | Unleashes venomous serpents |

# “Who Can Lift the Mighty Bow?"

With his yagna completed, Vishwamitra decided to take the princes to Mithila, ruled by King Janaka. On the way, he told them about the great bow of Lord Shiva kept there. “When Sita was a child, she once lifted the bow effortlessly, something no one else has ever done. Impressed by her strength, King Janaka announced a swayamvara. Only the man who can lift and string this bow shall marry Sita. Many princes tried, but all had failed.”

# “Mystery of the Divine Bow: Solve & Reveal”

***INSTRUCTIONS:*** The lord Shiva's bow has a name. To uncover this name, solve each puzzle below. Each correct answer will give you one letter of the word. Write the letter in the box after each puzzle.

| | Puzzle | Letter |
|---|---|---|
| 1 | Sage Vashishta advised Dasharatha to do which ritual?<br>Take First letter (Ex: Putrakameshti yagna ) | P |
| 2 | Unscramble this name: Take the second letter<br>A I W T H I A V S W M R | |
| 3 | Bharatha and ___ always played together<br>Take the second last letter | |
| 4 | What am I: Take the first letter.<br>This peaceful city was Rama's birthplace. | |
| 5 | After Dasharatha's Yagna, what did the fire god gave to Queens?<br>Take the first letter | |
| 6 | The word WEAPON in Sanskrit. Take the first letter | |

# “The Story of Ahalya"

As they neared Mithila, they saw an abandoned ashrama. Vishwamitra said, “This was once the home of Sage Gautama and his wife, Ahalya. She was tricked by Indra and cursed to become stone by her husband.” As Rama's foot made contact with the stone, Ahalya's curse decisively broke. With tears of gratitude, she bowed to Rama. Soon after, Sage Gautama returned, and they were joyfully reunited.

## “Complete Ahalya by finding missing piece.”

# “The Bow Contest and the wedding”

Soon they reached Mithila. The city was filled with excitement for the contest. Sita was returning from the temple. She saw Rama from a distance and thought, “He looks so noble and strong. I hope he wins.” The next day, many princes tried to lift the mighty bow but failed. Rama walked up calmly, lifted the bow with ease, and, as he pulled the string, it snapped in two with a loud crash! The crowd gasped in awe. Sita was extremely happy. She came forward and placed a garland around Rama’s neck. Their wedding was celebrated with great joy, and they returned to Ayodhya.

# "Half + Half = Whole!"

COMPLETE THESE PICTURES BY DRAWING THE OTHER HALF.

# "Manthara's Manipulation"

Years later, King Dasharatha decided to crown Rama as the next king. All of Ayodhya rejoiced, and even Queen Kaikeyi was happy at first. But her maid Manthara was furious. "Why should Rama be king? What about Bharata?" she asked. Kaikeyi replied, "Rama is brave and loved by all." Manthara manipulated Kaikeyi, "If Rama rules, your son will be forgotten. He will have no power, no place in the kingdom." She continued, "Use the two boons the king promised you." Slowly, Kaikeyi's heart filled with fear, and her joy turned into jealousy, worry, and anger.

## "Find the 13 differences & color"

# "Kaikeyi's Wishes"

Kaikeyi went to the Kopa Gruha, a special room for queens when they were upset. King Dasharatha rushed to her. "Kaikeyi! What's wrong? Tell me—I will do anything to make you smile!" Kaikeyi looked at him sadly, and said, "You promised me two wishes. I want to use them now. I want Rama to go to the forest for 14 years and Bharata to be king." The king was shocked. He tried to persuade her in every way he could, but she did not change her mind. The king was heartbroken and felt completely helpless.

# "Word Challenge"

***INSTRUCTIONS:*** Use the letters in **DASHARATHA** to make as many words as you can. Do not add extra letters which are not in the word. Example: star, hat

| | |
|---|---|
| ______________________ | ______________________ |
| ______________________ | ______________________ |
| ______________________ | ______________________ |
| ______________________ | ______________________ |
| ______________________ | ______________________ |
| ______________________ | ______________________ |

# “The Promise and the Farewell"

When Rama heard about the exile, he accepted it calmly and said, “I will gladly fulfill my father’s promise.” He went to inform his mother and Sita. They were shocked. Sita and Lakshmana insisted on going with him to the forest. Rama tried to stop them, but they wouldn’t listen. Finally, he agreed. Before leaving, he took blessings from his mothers. Kausalya hugged him and cried. Sumitra blessed them, saying, “Lakshmana, serve your brother with all your heart.” Kaikeyi was surprised by Rama’s calmness. He bowed before her and said, “I leave with your blessings and no anger in my heart.”

# “Find the hidden words”

**INSTRUCTIONS:** Words are hidden in these → ↓ ↘ directions. Can you find them?

| S | W | X | T | X | K | A | I | K | E | Y | I | H | A | P | P | Y | G |
|---|---|---|---|---|---|---|---|---|---|---|---|---|---|---|---|---|---|
| A | I | I | L | S | N | M | G | F | Y | E | U | Q | Q | I | F | Y | Z |
| Y | S | M | G | A | S | C | Z | F | O | X | A | N | G | E | R | R | B |
| D | H | R | F | M | A | N | T | H | A | R | A | E | G | U | K | T | J |
| G | E | U | P | F | D | A | S | I | T | A | E | R | C | E | F | M | B |
| V | S | B | M | Z | C | G | Z | K | X | W | X | S | A | Z | C | A | K |
| W | I | F | E | O | N | B | R | O | T | H | E | R | T | M | A | O | T |
| W | G | J | L | A | K | S | H | M | A | N | A | I | Q | H | A | V | O |
| B | H | A | R | A | T | H | A | R | T | M | K | I | N | G | P | E | A |
| Q | Q | X | A | C | F | Q | F | E | X | I | L | E | M | N | K | T | K |
| L | R | P | V | M | D | I | S | A | C | F | S | Q | G | S | C | Z | O |
| K | N | M | G | D | W | F | O | M | K | E | B | V | M | V | L | S | U |

ANGER
BHARATHA
BROTHER
EXILE
FOREST
HAPPY
KAIKEYI

SAD
SITA
WIFE
WISHES
KING
LAKSHMANA
MANTHARA
RAMA

# “Leaving Ayodhya Behind"

Rama, Sita, and Lakshmana wore simple clothes and bid farewell to their family. Sumantra, the minister, drove them out of Ayodhya in the chariot. The entire city was filled with sorrow and followed Rama. He asked them to return, but they refused. That night, everyone rested by the river Tamas. Early the next morning, before anyone woke up, Rama, Sita, Lakshmana, and Sumantra quietly continued their journey. When they reached the edge of the kingdom, Rama said, “Please return to Ayodhya and tell my father we are safe.” With tears, Sumantra bowed and returned to Ayodhya, while the three entered the forest to begin their new life.

# “Map Quest: Find the Places coordinates!”

**INSTRUCTIONS:** Look at the map with letter rows (A, B, C...) and number columns (1, 2, 3...). Find the place and write its grid box as a coordinate.

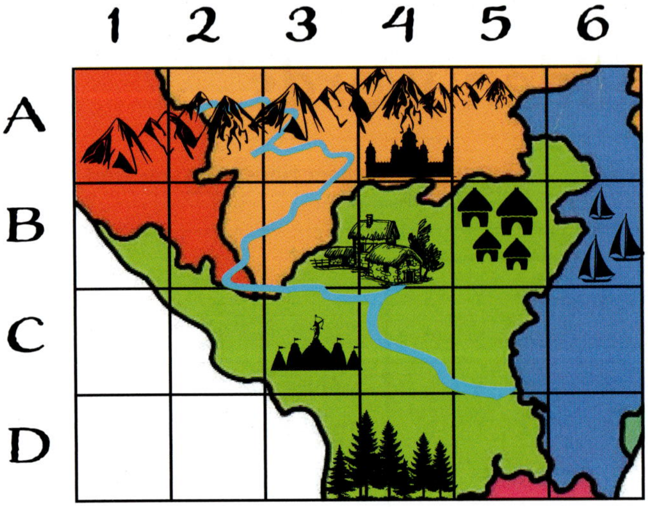

Example: Mountain - A1- A5

Mithila- ___________

Harbor-_____________

Ashram-___________

Ayodhya-___________

Village-____________

Forest-_____________

# "Rama & Guha's Friendship"

Rama, Sita, and Lakshmana traveled south until they reached the wide Ganga River. They didn't know how to cross it. Just then, they met Guha, the kind chief of the Nishada tribe. He was very happy to see them. "Rama! Please stay in my village. I will take care of everything," he said. Rama replied, "Thank you, Guha, but I must live in the forest. I have promised my father." Guha admired Rama and said, "Then let me help you cross the river." He arranged a boatman, who took them safely across. From there, they continued their journey and stayed in Chitrakoot for some time.

# "Find the 6 Differences"

# True or false

1.Guha was the chief of the Nishada tribe. TRUE FALSE

2.Rama, Sita, and Lakshmana crossed the Ganga River using a bridge. TRUE FALSE

3.Rama accepted Guha's offer to stay in the village. TRUE FALSE

4.They stayed in Chitrakoot after crossing the Ganga. TRUE FALSE

5.Sumantra also stayed with Rama. TRUE FALSE

# "Bharata's Loyalty"

Dasharatha was heartbroken without Rama and soon passed away. When Bharata returned to Ayodhya and found out about his father's death and Rama's exile, he was shocked and angry with his mother. "Rama should be king, not me!" he said. He went to the forest and begged Rama to return. But Rama replied, "I must keep my promise and stay for 14 years." Bharata accepted Rama's wish and placed Rama's sandals on the throne, vowing to rule in his name until he returned.

# "Rama's Padukas on the Throne!"

***INSTRUCTIONS:*** Join the dots to complete the picture of the Padukas, then let's color

# "A Visit to Sage Atri's Ashram"

After Bharata's departure, Rama, Lakshmana, and Sita left Chitrakoot and moved deeper into the Dandaka forest. On the way, they visited the ashram of Sage Atri and his wife, Anasuya. Anasuya was a kind and wise lady. She gifted Sita beautiful clothes and magical ornaments that would never get dirty. Sita accepted the gifts with deep gratitude.

## "Find the hidden objects"

***INSTRUCTIONS:*** Look at the picture below. Find these given objects in the picture.

# "Making the Forest Safe"

Rama, Sita, and Lakshmana continued their journey into the Dandaka Forest. It was vast and beautiful, but also filled with danger. Many demons troubled the sages living there. When the sages saw Rama, they asked him to protect them. For the next ten years, Rama and Lakshmana defeated many of these evil beings. Slowly, the forest became safe again. The sages were overjoyed and blessed Rama. Later, following Sage Agastya's advice, they continued their journey and settled in Panchavati, on the banks of the river Godavari.

# "Solve the maze to reach Panchavati"

### INSTRUCTIONS

1.Start at the first box (example: 3 × 3).
2.Solve the multiplication. (3 × 3 = 9)
3.Find the box next to it that has 9.
4.Solve the next multiplication near the number you found.
5.Keep solving and moving from box to box.
6.Find your way through the maze and reach the finish!

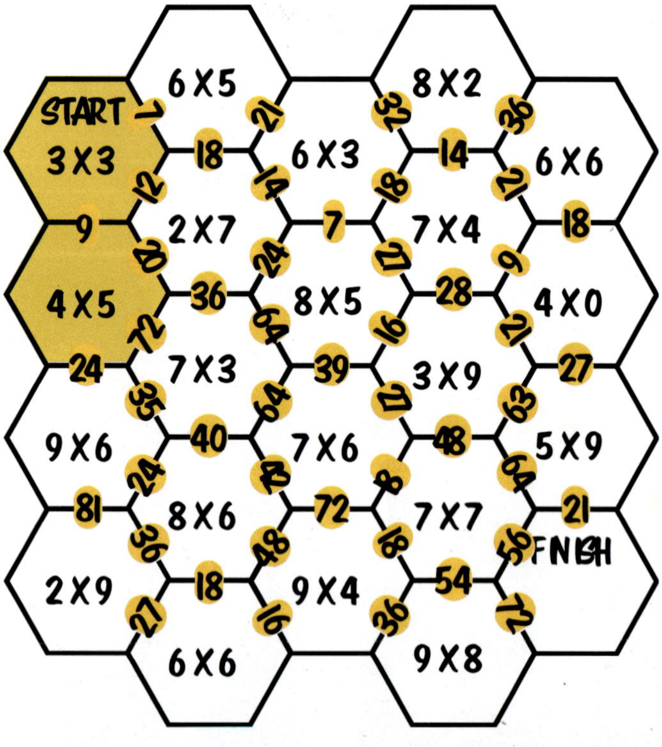

# "The Demoness in Disguise"

One day in the forest, the demoness Shurpanakha, sister of the demon king Ravana, came across Rama, Sita, and Lakshmana. Captivated by Rama's handsome appearance, she used her magical powers to turn into a beautiful woman and approached Rama. She praised his strength and said, "I am a better match for you than Sita. Marry me." But Rama, loyal to Sita, gently replied, "I am already married. But my brother Lakshmana is alone. His wife is not with him. Perhaps he might be interested in you."

## "Add Magic to Jewels!"

***INSTRUCTIONS:*** Use pattern and decorate the necklace

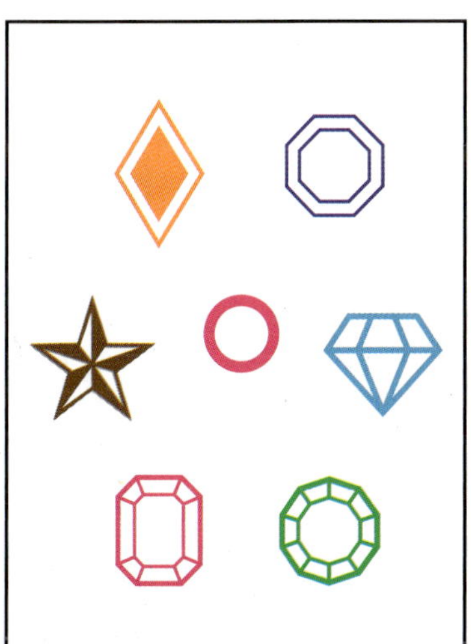

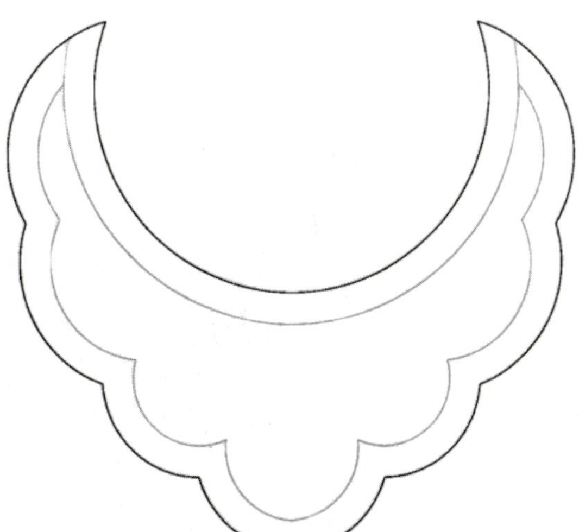

# "Lakshmana Protects Sita"

Shurpanakha approached Lakshmana and proposed marriage to him, but Lakshmana also teased and rejected her. Angry and humiliated, Shurpanakha saw Sita as the problem and attacked her. Before she could hurt Sita, Lakshmana quickly stopped her and, with his sword, cut off her nose and ears. Hurt and furious, Shurpanakha ran into the forest, planning revenge against Rama and Lakshmana.

## LET'S COLOR!

## “Ravana’s Wicked Plan"

Shurpanakha ran to her brother Ravana in Lanka, crying. “Oh, brother! Rama and Lakshmana hurt me! I only wanted to bring you the beautiful Sita, but they cut off my ears and nose. Only you deserve her!” Ravana became furious. He thought, “They dared to hurt my sister—and keep the woman meant for me?” Hearing about Sita’s beauty, Ravana decided to kidnap her. He called Maricha, a demon who could change shapes, and said, “Turn into a golden deer, and go near Rama, Sita, and Lakshmana’s hut.”

## “Dot by Dot-Spot the MagicalDeer!"

# "The Trick of the Golden Deer"

Maricha transformed himself into a beautiful golden deer and appeared near Rama's hut, catching the eye of Sita. Mesmerized by the magical creature, Sita insisted that Rama capture it for her. She wanted to keep it as a pet and later take it to Ayodhya. Lakshmana, however, grew suspicious. "Brother, this deer is no ordinary animal. It must be a trick of the demons," he warned. But Sita was adamant, and finally, Rama agreed. He instructed Lakshmana to stay with Sita and then followed the golden deer.

# "Where Did the Golden Deer Go?"

**HELP RAMA FIND THE SHIMMERING DEER HIDING DEEP IN THE FOREST!**

# "The Demon's Final Trick"

The golden deer ran farther into the forest, and Rama, determined to catch it, chased it deep into the jungle. Soon, he realized that it was no ordinary deer, but a demon in disguise. Rama took aim and shot it. As Maricha fell, his magical form disappeared. With his last breath, he cried out in Rama's voice, calling for Lakshmana to help him. The cry, filled with pain, echoed through the forest and reached the cottage where Sita and Lakshmana were waiting.

# "In the Forest: What Happened?"

***INSTRUCTIONS:*** Number the pictures from 1 to 4 to show what happened first, next, and last..

Lakshmana doubts the deer

Rama killed the deer

Rama chases the deer

Sita spots golden deer

# “The Lakshmana Rekha"

Sita heard Rama’s cry and grew worried. She urged Lakshmana to go help him. Lakshmana stayed calm and said, “Don’t worry, Mother. Brother is brave and powerful. That voice may be a demon’s trick.” But Sita insisted, “That was Rama! He needs you!” She pleaded him continuously. Though reluctant, Lakshmana finally agreed. Before leaving, he drew a glowing line around the hut with his arrow. “This Lakshmana Rekha will protect you. Please don’t step outside it.” Sita nodded, and with a heavy heart, Lakshmana went into the forest.

## “Complete the magic circle”

**INSTRUCTIONS:** Can you help Laksmna finish the circle around the hut?

# "Ravana's disguise"

As soon as Lakshmana left, Ravana appeared in the disguise of an old sage and tried to go near the hut. When he tried to cross the magical line, it burned him. Realizing he couldn't cross it, he called out for alms. Hearing the sage's voice, Sita came out with fruits and asked him to come inside. But Ravana pretended to be angry and said, "You are offering alms but not stepping out to give it? Do you want a sage's curse upon your husband?" Sita was confused. She had promised Lakshmana not to step out, but she didn't want to upset the sage. She thought, "A guest must be fed, it is ____________________." So, she slowly stepped out of the line.

# "Why Sita crossed the line?"

***INSTRUCTIONS:*** Look at the pictures below and then write the names of each picture in numerical order to complete the crossword to know the answer.

1 

2 

3 

4 

5 

6 

# "Sita's kidnap"

At that moment, Ravana revealed his true form. He grabbed her and carried her away in his Pushpaka Vimana, a magical flying chariot. Sita cried out, "Rama! Lakshmana!" as she struggled, but the chariot soared higher and higher into the sky. On their way, the great vulture Jatayu saw them and bravely tried to stop Ravana. Ravana struck Jatayu down with his sword, leaving the brave bird wounded. Sita, helpless and weeping, watched in horror. Ravana continued his flight and finally reached Lanka. There, he placed Sita in a beautiful but guarded garden called Ashoka Vatika. Sita sat beneath the Shimshapa tree, heartbroken and longing for Rama.

# "Find the 10 differences"

# "Jatayu's Last Words"

Back in the forest, Lakshmana found Rama safe and unharmed. Rama was surprised and asked, "Why did you leave Sita alone?" Lakshmana explained, and Rama immediately sensed something was wrong. Both ran back to the hut, but Sita was nowhere to be found. Filled with worry, they searched the forest, calling her name again and again. Soon, they came across Jatayu, lying on the ground badly wounded. Rama rushed to him and gently lifted his head. With great effort, Jatayu spoke his final words, "__________." Rama was deeply moved by Jatayu's bravery and sacrifice. With great respect, he performed Jatayu's last rites.

# "Solve the Cryptogram to decode Jatayu's message"

| A | B | C | D | E | F | G | H | I | J | K | L | M |
|---|---|---|---|---|---|---|---|---|---|---|---|---|
| 20 | 14 | 17 | 12 | 6 | 19 | 7 | 21 | 25 | 1 | 10 | 26 | 23 |

| N | O | P | Q | R | S | T | U | V | W | X | Y | Z |
|---|---|---|---|---|---|---|---|---|---|---|---|---|
| 2 | 3 | 15 | 22 | 13 | 5 | 16 | 8 | 18 | 24 | 11 | 4 | 9 |

### HOW TO FIND THE HIDDEN MESSAGE.

1. Each letter has been replaced by a number.
2. Decode the message by figuring out which letter corresponds to which number.
3. Eg: 13 20 23 20 is R A M A.

__ __ __ __ __ __   __ __ __ __   __ __ __ __   __ __
13 20 18 20 2 20   16 3 3 10   5 25 16 20   16 3

__ __ __ __ __   __   __ __ __ __ __   __ __
26 20 2 10 20   25   16 13 25 6 12   16 3

__ __ __ __   __ __ __ ,   __ __ __   __ __
5 16 3 15   21 25 23 ,   14 8 16   21 6

__ __ __ __ __ __   __ __   __ __ __ __ .
5 16 13 8 17 10   23 6   12 3 24 2 .

# "Shabari's Long Wait"

Both continued their journey southward and reached a peaceful hermitage by the banks of Pampa Lake. This was the ashram of a kind and humble old tribal woman named Shabari. She had come to the forest to serve and learn from the great sage Rishi Matanga. Before his death, the sage had told her, "One day, Lord Rama himself will visit you. Serve him and direct him to find Sugriva." Since then, Shabari waited patiently every day.

## "Devotion Jar: What Would You Offer with Love?"

**INSTRUCTIONS:** Shabari offered sweet berries to Rama with great love. Think of things you would offer to Lord Rama. Write or draw them inside the jar below.

# "The Path to Sugriva"

When Rama finally arrived, Shabari was overwhelmed with joy. She offered him berries, tasting each one first to make sure it was sweet. She did it with love, not knowing it was something people usually shouldn't do. Rama gratefully accepted the fruits. He said, "Shabari, your love and devotion make these fruits sweeter than anything else." Rama's kind words made her heart bloom with happiness. Shabari then guided Rama and Lakshmana toward the Rishyamukha mountain, where they would find Sugriva, the exiled vanara prince, and a group of capable vanaras. Taking Shabari's advice, Rama and Lakshmana made their way to Rishyamukha.

## "Help Rama, Lakshmana reach Rishyamukha"

# What Happens Next?

Will Rama meet the monkey prince Sugriva???
Will Rama find Sita and defeat the mighty Ravana???
Where is Hanuman???

Join us in Part 2 for more adventures, surprises, and exciting activities from the Ramayana!

Did you enjoy these puzzles and activities? Would you like to get 10 printable worksheets for free? It's easy! Just leave a review of this book on Amazon, Flipkart, or our social media page. Take a screenshot of your review, and email it to me at

**akshatasaibaba@gmail.com**

I will **email** you your free worksheets as a **thank you!** I can't wait to hear from you — and I hope you had as much fun reading and solving as I had creating this book for you!

# ANSWERS

## YAGNA TIME

## FILL IN THE BLANKS

1.Vishwamitra 2.Rama 3. Lakshmana

4. Maricha and Subahu 5. Sage Vashishta

## WHY SITA CROSSED THE LINE?
DHARMA

## TRUE OR FALSE
T,F,F,T,F

## DIVINE GIIFTS TO RAMA

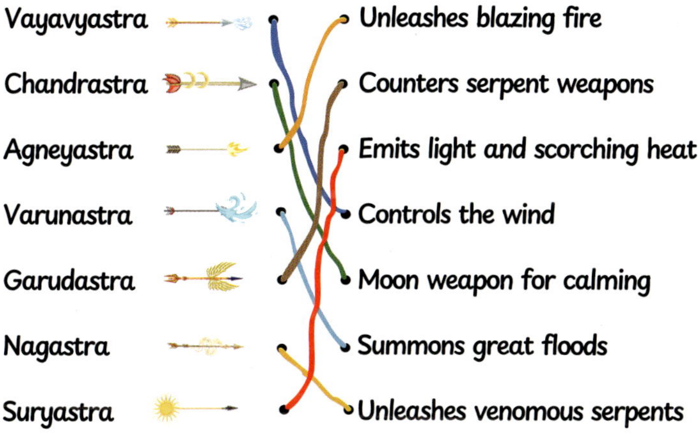


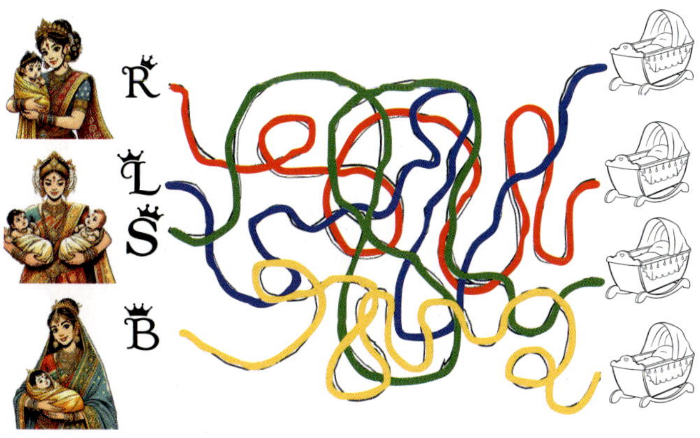


## IN THE FOREST: WHAT HAPPENED?

4, 1, 3, 2

## MYSTERY BOW- PINAKA
## AHALYA'S MISSING PIECES-1,2,5

## WORD CHALLENGE

hat, rat, ash, had, art, dash, rash, dart, hats, trash, harsh, data,

| | | | | | | | | | | | | | | | | | |
|---|---|---|---|---|---|---|---|---|---|---|---|---|---|---|---|---|---|
| S | W | X | T | X | K | A | I | K | E | Y | I | H | A | P | P | Y | G |
| A | I | I | L | S | N | M | G | F | Y | E | U | Q | Q | I | F | Y | Z |
| Y | S | M | G | A | S | C | Z | F | O | X | A | N | G | E | R | R | B |
| D | H | R | F | M | A | N | T | H | A | R | A | E | G | U | K | T | J |
| G | E | U | P | F | D | A | S | I | T | A | E | R | C | E | F | M | B |
| V | S | B | M | Z | C | G | Z | K | X | W | X | S | A | Z | C | A | K |
| W | I | F | E | O | N | B | R | O | T | H | E | R | T | M | A | O | T |
| W | G | J | L | A | K | S | H | M | A | N | A | I | Q | H | A | V | O |
| B | H | A | R | A | T | H | A | R | T | M | K | I | N | G | P | E | A |
| Q | Q | X | A | C | F | Q | F | E | X | I | L | E | M | N | K | T | K |
| L | R | P | V | M | D | I | S | A | C | F | S | Q | G | S | C | Z | O |
| K | N | M | G | D | W | F | O | M | K | E | B | V | M | V | L | S | U |

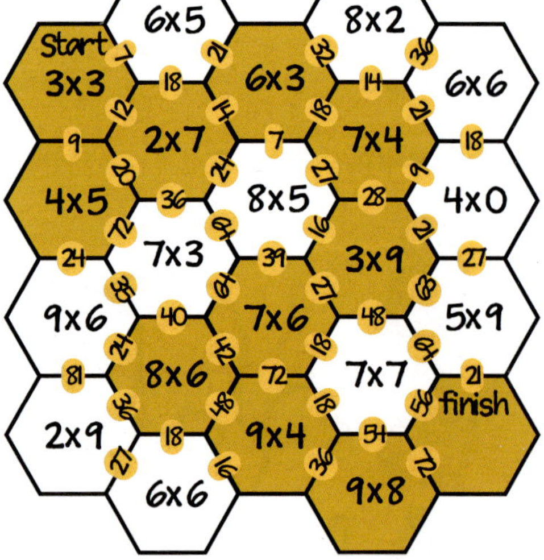


**CRYPTOGRAM:** Ravana took Sita to Lanka. I tried to stop him, but he struck me down.